WRITING PROMPTS WORKBOOK

GRADES

Story Starters, Writing Prompts, Grammar and Vocabulary.

Founded in 2017, Thomas Media is a publisher of gift books, creative books, innovative journals, cards, notepads and stationery. Thomas Media publishes over 50 books and ancillary products per year.

© Thomas Media

Visit us at Thomasmedia.ie

Copyright © 2020
by Thomas Media Ltd.
Athlone, Westmeath, Ireland
All Rights Reserved

ISBN: 978-1-913366-34-6
Printed: United States

"Writing Prompts Workbook" © Thomas Media Limited 2020. All rights reserved. No part of this kit shall be reproduced, stored in a retrieval system, or transmitted by any means – electronic, mechanical, photocopying, recording, or otherwise – without written permission from the publisher.

TABLE OF CONTENTS

WRITING PROMPTS

Chapter 1 - HOLIDAY TIME 4
Chapter 2 - ANIMALS AND PETS 14
Chapter 3 - FRIENDS 24
Chapter 4 - CARTOON CHARACHTERS 34
Chapter 5 - EVERYBODY LOVES ART 44
Chapter 6 - TELEVISION ADVERTS 54
Chapter 7 - SEASONS AND WEATHER 64
Chapter 8 - SCHOOL TIMES 74
Chapter 9 - PARENTS AND THE HOME 84
Chapter 10 - SPORTS AND ATHLETES 94

BUILDING BLOCKS

Chapter 11 - VOCABULARY BUILDER 104
Chapter 12 - GRAMMAR BUILDER 108
Chapter 13 - STORY BUILDER 120

GRADES

What holiday makes you the happiest? Why?

Do you think there should be a Children's Day?

How can we honor veterans on Veteran's Day?

Do students receive enough time off for Christmas holidays?

CHAPTER 1: HOLIDAY TIME

How does your family celebrate the new year?

Is it fair for adults to scare children on Halloween?

CHAPTER 1: HOLIDAY TIME

Should children receive books as Christmas gifts?

Are parents too old to wear Halloween costumes? What do you think?

Tell about your least favorite Christmas gift. Why were you disappointed?

What do you normally do on Thanksgiving? Tell about family games, food, and more!

What does your family do on Easter?

What is the best gift a father could receive on Father's Day?

What is the best gift a mother could receive on Mother's Day?

_____
_____
_____
_____
_____
_____
_____

What is the worst gift a father could receive on Father's Day?

_____
_____
_____
_____
_____
_____
_____

What is the worst gift a mother could receive on Mother's Day?

What is your favorite Christmas gift? Why was it your favorite?

What is your least favorite holiday? What happened to make it your least favorite?

Why do some people dislike Halloween?

Why do you like or dislike Halloween?

_____
_____
_____
_____
_____
_____
_____
_____

Would you rather dress up as a scary monster or Mickey Mouse?

_____
_____
_____
_____
_____
_____
_____
_____

What can having a pet teach you?

What is your favorite animal?

Do you think dogs can communicate with one another? Why?

How can adults protect wild animals like tigers and bears?

How do you think ants feel about humans?

How old should you be to receive a pet?

If birds could speak English, what would they say?

If you could choose, would you rather be a squirrel or a rabbit?

If you could make up an imaginary animal, what would it be? Describe the animal's face and body.

Imagine there was one pet left on Earth. Who should receive it?

Should all teachers be required to own pets? Why or why not?

Should everyone own at least one pet? Why or why not?

Do you think a snake would be a good pet or should they be left in the wild?

Do you think it's easy or hard to care for a pet?

Why do some people avoid having pets?

What animal scares you the most?

What animal would make a good pet?

What animal would make a great class pet?

What animal would not make a great class pet?

Should hospital allow pets to room with patients?

Can having friends make you happy?

_____
_____
_____
_____
_____
_____

How can you encourage your friend to make good choices?

_____
_____
_____
_____
_____
_____
_____

How can you support your friends? Do friends always agree?

If a friend is mean to you, what is the best way to handle it?

If you had to choose between Frosty the Snowman or Olaf, which one would you choose to be your best friend?

_____
_____
_____
_____
_____
_____
_____

If your friend was a bully, what would you do?

_____
_____
_____
_____
_____
_____
_____
_____

Is it better to have one great friend or several good friends?

Is it tough to be a good friend? Why or why not?

Is it your responsibility to protect your friend from bullies?

Should parents have the right to choose your friends?

What are some lessons that you have learned from previous friendships?

What can you teach others about being a good friend?

Why should you be nice to your friends?

When is it time to end a friendship?

Would you feel bad about ending a friendship?

Write about a time when you and your friend had an argument.

What field trip would you like to take with your friend?

_____
_____
_____
_____
_____
_____
_____

What qualities make a good friend?

_____
_____
_____
_____
_____
_____
_____

What would you do if your friend was about to make a bad choice?

How would you encourage your friends if they felt sad?

Write about your favorite cartoon character.

Why do you think most cartoons are played on Saturday morning?

Cartoon characters often do silly things. Write about a time when you did a silly thing

How can cartoons encourage small children to make bad choices?

How many cartoons should small children be allowed to view in a day?

_____
_____
_____
_____
_____
_____
_____

If you could become a cartoon character, which one would it be and why?

_____
_____
_____
_____
_____
_____
_____

If you could design your own cartoon character, what would it look like?

Should adults watch cartoons?

Should parents have to watch cartoons with their children?

How can cartoons teach a lesson?

What cartoon character regularly makes bad choices?

What cartoon character would you like to invite to dinner? Why?

What if Mickey Mouse became a real person? Where would he live and what job could he perform?

_____
_____
_____
_____
_____
_____
_____

What if your parents could adopt a cartoon character? Who should it be and why?

_____
_____
_____
_____
_____
_____
_____

What superhero would not make a good cartoon character?

What five cartoon characters would make a great basketball team?

What five cartoon characters would not make a great basketball team?

Write about a funny scene from your favorite cartoon show.

Write about a scary scene from a cartoon show?

Write about how you would defeat an evil cartoon character.

CHAPTER 4: CARTOON CHARACTERS

Do you think anyone can be an artist? Why or why not?

Do you think anyone can make money selling art?

Do you think graffiti is art?

Do you think some people take art too seriously?

Do you think you are a great artist?

_____
_____
_____
_____
_____
_____

Have you ever been to an art gallery? If so, tell about your visit. If not, would you like to go?

_____
_____
_____
_____
_____
_____

How can art can show a person's feelings?

How is art different from other school subjects?

If you could create a sculpture, what type would you create?

Is art an important subject in school?

Should schools allow students to attend art classes?

Someone is going to pay you $1,000 to draw a picture. What will you draw?

What types of art do you like?

Which is better: a painting or a photo?

Which is better: a sculpture or a painting?

Why do some students perform well in art and others don't?

Would you rather have a photo of yourself or a painting?

Would you rather make pottery or draw a picture?

Write about your favorite artist.

Write about your favorite picture.

Write about your favorite television ad.

Write about your least favorite television ad.

Do you see more men or women in television ads?

Do you think parents should allow their children to advertise products on television?

Do you think some television ads are inappropriate for little children?

Do you think some television ads hide the entire truth about a product?

Do you think television ads influence your parents to buy things?

Do you think too many television ads are shown everyday?

Do you think you could sell things on television? Would you be nervous?

_____
_____
_____
_____
_____
_____
_____

Have you ever seen a television ad that didn't make sense? Tell about it.

_____
_____
_____
_____
_____
_____
_____
_____

How are some television ads different from others?

If someone asked you to write a negative television ad, would you do it?

If you were asked to create an ad to showcase your school, what would it say?

If you could write a funny television ad for a new toy, what would it say?

If you were asked to write a serious television ad about an animal, which animal would you choose?

_____
_____
_____
_____
_____
_____

Should famous people sell things on television? Why would you choose that animal?

_____
_____
_____
_____
_____
_____

What if there were more television ads than television shows? How would people feel about it?

What makes a good television ad? How do advertisers get people to buy products?

Do your parents ever complain about television ads?

Would you buy something just because a celebrity was advertising it?

Are you afraid of thunderstorms? Why or why not?

_____
_____
_____
_____
_____
_____
_____
_____

Do you think schools should open during the summer?

_____
_____
_____
_____
_____
_____
_____
_____

If you could pick a place to live during the summer, where would it be?

If you could pick a place to live during the winter, where would it be?

If you could teach a class about weather safety, would you rather teach teenagers or small children?

_____
_____
_____
_____
_____
_____

Should all schools close if there's a snowstorm?

_____
_____
_____
_____
_____
_____
_____

What is your favorite thing about fall?

What is your favorite thing about summer?

What is your favorite thing about winter?

What is your favorite thing about spring?

What is your favorite thing to do on a rainy day?

What is your least favorite thing about fall?

What is your least favorite thing about summer?

What is your least favorite thing about winter?

What is your least favorite thing about spring?

What would you do to prepare for a hurricane?

What's the main difference between summer and spring?

Why is it important to take shelter during a lightning storm?

Would you ever play in the rain for fun?

Write about your favorite place to visit in the summer?

Write about a time when you received an award or special recognition.

Write about your favorite teacher. Tell why he or she is your favorite.

Do you think school bullies should be given another chance?

In 2019, most students are required to go to school at least 170 days. How many days do you think students should go to school each year?

Is it fair to require all students to wear a school uniform?

Is it important for all students to take art and music?

Should parents have the right to sit in their child's classroom?

Should physical education be required of all students

Should students go to school year round?

Should students keep the same teacher for first through fifth grade?

Should teachers be required to take the same tests as students?

Should the state require all 4 year olds to attend preschool?

What can be done to help bullies realize their mistakes?

What if you could read to every 1st grade class in your school? What would you read and why?

What if you were told that you were retained? How would you react?

What subjects school be removed from the school day?

What subjects should be added to the school day?

What's your favorite subject?

What's your least favorite subject?

Write about a time when you had fun in class.

At what age should children be allowed to pick their own outfits?

At what age should children be allowed to stay at a friend's house?

Describe a time when you were surprised by your parents?

Describe a typical Saturday at your home.

Do you believe that all parents should make their children go to college?

If you could take a dream family vacation, where would you go?

Is it fair to make siblings share a bedroom?

Should all siblings be treated equally?

Should parents allow their children to set their own bedtime?

Should parents and children write household rules together?

Should parents have the right to confront school bullies?

What are three things every grandparent should know about their grandchildren?

What are three things every mom should know about their children?

What are three things every dad should know about their children?

What special traditions are present in your family?

What's a typical day like in your family?

Why is it important to behave for your parents?

_____
_____
_____
_____
_____
_____
_____

Would you rather ride a rollercoaster with your parents or with your friends? Explain.

_____
_____
_____
_____
_____
_____
_____

Write about a time when you got in trouble. How did you feel?

Write about a time when your parents praised you for doing something right. How did it make you feel? What did you learn?

Would you rather be a professional basketball player or a professional soccer player? Why?

Write a letter to your favorite athlete

Do you think professional athletes should be paid hivher than average wages for sports?

Do you think baseball players work as hard as football players?

CHAPTER 10: SPORTS AND ATHLETES

Do you think professional athletes are role models?

Do you think professional athletes should visit hospitals?

Do you think tennis players work as hard as basketball players?

Have you ever met a professional athlete? If so, tell about it. If not, would you like to meet? What would you talk about?

If you could play against one professional athlete, who would it be?

_____
_____
_____
_____
_____
_____
_____

Should athletes be allowed to do a victory dance after winning a game?

_____
_____
_____
_____
_____
_____
_____

Should professional athletes be required to donate to charities?

Should professional athletes be required to sign autographs after a game?

Should professional skaters be allowed to judge their competitors?

What professional athlete do you admire?

What professional athlete should visit your school? Why?

What sport is equires more skill to play: tennis or volleyball?

Who are you two least favorite professional athletes?

Who are your favorite female athletes?

Who are your favorite male athletes?

Why is it important for professional athletes to give back to their communities?

VOCABULARY BUILDER 1ST GRADE

For this exercise, you are required to research the following words, discover the meaning of each word and ultimately, use the word in your writing. Once you have used each word three times, cross the word from your list. This is a great exercise to repeat later.

TICK A BOX EVERY TIME YOU USES THESE WORDS

annoy	☐	☐	☐	question	☐	☐	☐
ignore	☐	☐	☐	curious	☐	☐	☐
prefer	☐	☐	☐	jealous	☐	☐	☐
attention	☐	☐	☐	reminds	☐	☐	☐
instead	☐	☐	☐	curve	☐	☐	☐
problem	☐	☐	☐	leader	☐	☐	☐
calm	☐	☐	☐	repeat	☐	☐	☐
investigate	☐	☐	☐	decide	☐	☐	☐
protect	☐	☐	☐	list	☐	☐	☐
comfortable	☐	☐	☐	report	☐	☐	☐
invite	☐	☐	☐	directions	☐	☐	☐
proud	☐	☐	☐	listen	☐	☐	☐
consequences	☐	☐	☐	rhyme	☐	☐	☐
important	☐	☐	☐	discover	☐	☐	☐

lovely	☐	☐	☐	fascinating	☐	☐	☐
respect	☐	☐	☐	note	☐	☐	☐
disappointed	☐	☐	☐	suggestion	☐	☐	☐
measuring	☐	☐	☐	feast	☐	☐	☐
searching	☐	☐	☐	notice	☐	☐	☐
embarrassed	☐	☐	☐	surprise	☐	☐	☐
miserable	☐	☐	☐	focus	☐	☐	☐
special	☐	☐	☐	observing	☐	☐	☐
enormous	☐	☐	☐	uncomfortable	☐	☐	☐
mumble	☐	☐	☐	frustrated	☐	☐	☐
spotless	☐	☐	☐	opposite	☐	☐	☐
exhausted	☐	☐	☐	warning	☐	☐	☐
negative	☐	☐	☐	gigantic	☐	☐	☐
squirm	☐	☐	☐	ordinary	☐	☐	☐
explore	☐	☐	☐	wonder	☐	☐	☐
nervous	☐	☐	☐	grumpy	☐	☐	☐
stomped	☐	☐	☐	positive	☐	☐	☐
fair	☐	☐	☐	worried	☐	☐	☐
nibbled	☐	☐	☐	huge	☐	☐	☐
suddenly	☐	☐	☐	precious	☐	☐	☐

VOCABULARY BUILDER 2ND GRADE

For this exercise, you are required to research the following words, discover the meaning of each word and ultimately, use the word in your writing. Once you have used each word three times, cross the word from your list. This is a great exercise to repeat later.

TICK A BOX EVERY TIME YOU USES THESE WORDS

amaze	☐	☐	☐	peeking	☐	☐	☐
energy	☐	☐	☐	avoid	☐	☐	☐
non-living	☐	☐	☐	expect	☐	☐	☐
amusing	☐	☐	☐	plan	☐	☐	☐
emormous	☐	☐	☐	cause	☐	☐	☐
noticed	☐	☐	☐	famous	☐	☐	☐
analyze	☐	☐	☐	poke	☐	☐	☐
escape	☐	☐	☐	flock	☐	☐	☐
observed	☐	☐	☐	predict	☐	☐	☐
annoy	☐	☐	☐	community	☐	☐	☐
estimate	☐	☐	☐	friendly	☐	☐	☐
opinion	☐	☐	☐	prefer	☐	☐	☐
arranged	☐	☐	☐	conclusion	☐	☐	☐
exercise	☐	☐	☐	frighten	☐	☐	☐

process	☐	☐	☐	detail	☐	☐	☐
connection	☐	☐	☐	investigate	☐	☐	☐
frown	☐	☐	☐	diagram	☐	☐	☐
publish	☐	☐	☐	suppose	☐	☐	☐
continue	☐	☐	☐	difference	☐	☐	☐
gasp	☐	☐	☐	leaned	☐	☐	☐
records	☐	☐	☐	sway	☐	☐	☐
cooperation	☐	☐	☐	different	☐	☐	☐
gather	☐	☐	☐	living	☐	☐	☐
revise	☐	☐	☐	stormy	☐	☐	☐
curious	☐	☐	☐	discover	☐	☐	☐
gust	☐	☐	☐	march	☐	☐	☐
separate	☐	☐	☐	swoop	☐	☐	☐
cycle	☐	☐	☐	drowsy	☐	☐	☐
steaming	☐	☐	☐	matter	☐	☐	☐
include	☐	☐	☐	treasure	☐	☐	☐
shivered	☐	☐	☐	moist	☐	☐	☐
describe	☐	☐	☐	vanish	☐	☐	☐
insist	☐	☐	☐	necessary	☐	☐	☐
similar	☐	☐	☐	volunteer	☐	☐	☐

GRAMMAR BUILDER

For this exercise, you are required to identify the noun. Some statements may have more than one noun.
SELECT THE CORRECT ANSWER(S) FROM THE OPTIONS BELOW.

1. Shower must be broken.

a) Shower
b) must
c) be
d) broken
Answer:_____

2. Lauren went to him.

a) Lauren
b) went
c) to
d) him
Answer:_____

3. Her hopes were lost.

a) hopes
b) Her
c) were
d) Lost
Answer:_____

4. His face turned pale.

a) face
b) pale
c) His
d) turned
Answer:_____

5. Simon began to shake.

a) Simon
b) began
c) to
d) shake
Answer:_____

6. A penalty must be given.

a) penalty
b) must
c) be
d) given
Answer:_____

7. No Peter was there.

a) Peter
b) No
c) was
d) there
Answer:_____

8. Matt picked it up.

a) Matt
b) picked
c) it
d) up
Answer:_____

9. The sky was blue.

a) sky
b) The
c) was
d) blue
Answer:_____

10. Robin began to sing.

a) Robin
b) began
c) to
d) sing
Answer:_____

11. Joe could not speak.

a) Joe
b) could
c) not
d) speak
Answer:_____

12. Her daughters paid for her.

a) daughters
b) Her
c) paid
d) for
Answer:_____

13. The Cowboy got on his horse.

a) horse
b) Cowboy
c) got
d) on
Answer:_____

14. School was better than that.

a) School
b) was
c) better
d) than
Answer:_____

15. His clothes were very torn.

a) clothes
b) His
c) were
d) very
Answer:_____

ANSWERS
1. Shower
2. Lauren
3. hopes
4. face, pale
5. Simon
6. Penalty
7. Peter
8. Matt
9. sky
10. Robin
11. Joe
12. daughters
13. horse, Cowboy
14. School
15. clothes

GRAMMAR BUILDER

In this exercise we will focus on Action Verbs. Identify the Action Verbs from the given options.

1. He began to sing.

a) Began
b) sing
c) to
d) He
Answer:_____

2. Paul began to cry.

a) Paul
b) egan
c) to
d) cry
Answer:_____

3. Listen to the noise.

a) Listen
b) to
c) the
d) noise
Answer:_____

4. Look at the big dog.

a) Look
b) at
c) big
d) dog
Answer:_____

5. Simon began to fall.

a) Simon
b) began
c) to
d) fall
Answer:_____

6. The journey slowly passed.

a) journey
b) the
c) slowly
d) passed
Answer:_____

7. Paul paid the shop keeper.

a) Paul
b) paid
c) shop
d) keeper
Answer:_____

8. We heard them singing.

a) We
b) heard
c) them
d) singing
Answer:_____

9. His son talked camly to him.

a) son
b) talked
c) him
d) calmy
Answer:_____

10. Robin laughed and cried.

a) Robin
b) laughed
c) and
d) cried
Answer:_____

11. Joe was moving fast.

a) Joe
b) moving
c) was
d) fast
Answer:_____

12. Sarah was shaking with fear.

a) Sarah
b) shaking
c) with
d) fear
Answer:_____

13. The Cowboy tried to climb.

a) the
b) Cowboy
c) tried
d) climb
Answer:_____

14. Paul wanted to try.

a) Paul
b) wanted
c) to
d) try
Answer:_____

15. He though of telling the truth.

a) though
b) of
c) telling
d) truth
Answer:_____

ANSWERS

1. Sing, began
2. cry, began
3. listen
4. Look
5. began, fall
6. passed
7. paid
8. heard, singing
9. talked
10. laughed, cried
11. moving
12. shaking, fear
13. tried, climb
14. wanted, try
15. thought, telling

GRAMMAR BUILDER

In this exercise we will focus on Adjetives. Identify the Adjetives from the given options.

1. Paul was never wrong.

a) Paul
b) was
c) never
d) wrong
Answer:_____

2. Paul was still free.

a) Paul
b) was
c) still
d) free
Answer:_____

3. Louise was very ill.

a) Louise
b) was
c) very
d) ill
Answer:_____

4. Peter was still very sad.

a) Peter
b) still
c) very
d) sad
Answer:_____

5. Simon was very weak.

a) Simon
b) was
c) very
d) weak
Answer:_____

6. His face grew bright.

a) His
b) face
c) grew
d) bright
Answer:_____

7. The man was very rich.

a) man
b) was
c) very
d) rich
Answer:_____

8. It made her happy.

a) It
b) made
c) her
d) happy
Answer:_____

9. His son felt very sick.

a) son
b) felt
c) very
d) sick
Answer:_____

10. The night was very dark.

a) night
b) was
c) very
d) dark
Answer:_____

11. The water was so deep.

a) water
b) was
c) so
d) deep
Answer:_____

12. The man was big and large.

a) man
b) was
c) big
d) large
Answer:_____

13. The door was to small.

a) the
b) door
c) was
d) small
Answer:_____

14. The path was narrow and dark.

a) path
b) was
c) narrow
d) dark
Answer:_____

15. She has great wit.

a) she
b) has
c) great
d) wit
Answer:_____

ANSWERS
1. mad
2. free
3. ill
4. sad
5. weak
6. bright
7. rich
8. happy
9. sick
10. dark
11. deep
12. big, large
13. small
14. narrow, dark
15. wit

GRAMMAR BUILDER

In this exercise we will focus on the Present Tense. Identify the present tense from the lists below.

1. Yet, he went to them expecting.

a) expecting
b) Yet
c) he
d) went
Answer:_____

2. The cars begin to drive north.

a) cars
b) begin
c) drive
d) north
Answer:_____

3. I wanted him to forget me.

a) wanted
b) him
c) forget
d) me
Answer:_____

4. She paused to look at her.

a) She
b) look
c) paused
d) her
Answer:_____

5. It is time we begin to think.

a) think
b) time
c) we
d) begin
Answer:_____

6. Moving from left to right.

a) moving
b) from
c) left
d) right
Answer:_____

7. The man tried to get caught.

a) get
b) The
c) man
d) tried
Answer:_____

8. She told the dog to go outside.

a) go
b) She
c) told
d) dog
Answer:_____

9. Then she went home to sleep.

a) sleep
b) Then
c) she
d) went
Answer:_____

10. Again, Matt began to ache.

a) ache
b) Again
c) Matt
d) began
Answer:_____

11. He at on the chair dreaming.

a) dreaming
b) He
c) sat
d) on
Answer:_____

12. Now Paul tried pushing Josh.

a) pushing
b) Now
c) Paul
d) tried
Answer:_____

13. They found more water to drink.

a) drink
b) They
c) caught
d) more
Answer:_____

14. Peter wanted to try, also.

a) try
b) Peter
c) wanted
d) to
Answer:_____

15. A little snow began to fall.

a) fall
b) A
c) little
d) snow
Answer:_____

ANSWERS
1. expecting
2. drive
3. forget
4. look
5. think
6. moving
7. get
8. go
9. eat
10. ache
11. dreaming
12. pushing
13. drink
14. try
15. fall

GRAMMAR BUILDER

In this exercise we will focus on the Present Tense. Identify the future tense from the lists below.

1. He will return someday

a) will
b) He
c) wil returnl
d) return
Answer:_____

2. He will call out the dates.

a) will call
b) He
c) will
d) dates
Answer:_____

3. Thousands will follow the music .

a) will
b) Thousands
c) follow
d) will follow
Answer:_____

4. We will build a fantastic team.

a) a) will build
b) We
c) fantastic

d) will
Answer:_____

5. I will present a gift to her.

a) will present
b) I
c) will
d) present
Answer:_____

6. I will let him sulk quietly.

a) I
b) will let
c) will
d) let
Answer:_____

7. This will be a great adventure.

a) be
b) This
c) will
d) will be
Answer:_____

8. Other men will be along soon.

a) Other
b) will be
c) men
d) will
Answer:_____

9. Do not lift that box

a) Do not
b) Do
c) lift
d) not
Answer:_____

10. The flowers will grow again.

a) will grow
b) flowers
c) grow
d) will
Answer:_____

11. The children will come alone.

a) will come
b) The
c) will
d) come
Answer:_____

12. I will find you!.

a) will catch
b) I
c) will
d) catch
Answer:_____

13. This will take only a second.

a) will take
b) This
c) will
d) take
Answer:_____

14. I will run for president.

a) will run
b) I
c) will
d) president
Answer:_____

15. They will bake some cakes.

a) They will
b) will bake
c) will
d) cakes
Answer:_____

ANSWERS
1. will return
2. will call
3. will follow
4. will build
5. will present
6. will let
7. will be
8. will be
9. do not
10. will grow
11. will come
12. will find
13. will take
14. will run
15. will bake

GRAMMAR BUILDER

In this exercise we will focus on Comparative Adjetives. Identify the Comparative Adjetives from the given options.

1. He thinks you are less than fair.

a) fair
b) thinks
c) less
d) are
Answer:_____

2. Paul was bigger than the box.

a) Paul
b) was
c) than
d) bigger
Answer:_____

3. Oh, if they had but been smarter!

a) had
b) they
c) smarter
d) been
Answer:_____

4. There is little more to say about it.

a) little
b) more
c) there
d) about
Answer:_____

5. His step was growing smaller.

a) His
b) step
c) smaller
d) growing
Answer:_____

6. She had less to think about.

a) She
b) less
c) think
d) about
Answer:_____

7. The man was more than rich.

a) than
b) was
c) more
d) rich
Answer:_____

8. He earned five dollars more.

a) He
b) earned
c) five
d) more
Answer:_____

9. His son was now stronger.

a) son
b) now
c) was
d) stronger
Answer:_____

10. You have better hair than me.

a) have
b) better
c) hair
d) than
Answer:_____

11. In less than a second it fell.

a) less
b) second
c) fell
d) than
Answer:_____

12. The man was taller than him.

a) man
b) was
c) taller
d) than
Answer:_____

13. The road had seemed longer.

a) the
b) road
c) seemed
d) longer
Answer:_____

14. The girl was smaller than him.

a) girl
b) was
c) smaller
d) than
Answer:_____

15. It would be better to run now.

a) run
b) better
c) would
d) now
Answer:_____

ANSWERS
1. less
2. bigger
3. smarter
4. more
5. smaller
6. less
7. more
8. more
9. stronger
10. better
11. less
12. taller
13. longer
14. smaller
15. better

Story Time: What holiday makes you the happiest? Why?

Story Time: Write a story about the coolest place you ever went to. Why did you like it so much?

Story Time: Write a story about your grandparents. What is your favorite thing to do with them?

Story Time: Write about a time when you got to do something fun that only kids can do. How do you think your parents felt?

Story Time: Write about a time when you made a new friend. How did you meet him or her?

Story Time: Write about a time you went on an adventure? Who was with you? Where did you go? What did you discover? How did you feel?

www.ingramcontent.com/pod-product-compliance
Lightning Source LLC
Chambersburg PA
CBHW081351080526
44588CB00016B/2459